The Big Band Drummer

A Complete Workbook For Improving Big Band Drumming Performance

By Ron Spagnardi

Design And Layout By Joe King

Published By
Modern Drummer Publications, Inc.
12 Old Bridge Road
Cedar Grove, NJ 07009 USA

Table of Contents

Introduction

Performing in a big band, and accurately interpreting a big band drum part, can present a challenge to beginning and experienced drummers alike. **The Big Band Drummer** has been written and designed specifically to help drummers better understand the intricacies of this specialized form of drumming. Time notation, section and ensemble figures, phrasing, and fill-ins are all thoroughly discussed, and a wealth of practice examples are included to help you improve your big band drumming performance.

Bear in mind that the typical big band drum chart is, for the most part, just a basic outline that includes time signature and tempo markings, and hopefully the style of the arrangement (rock, jazz, Latin). Many arrangers also write in dynamics, along with cues that detail which sections of the band are playing during the arrangement (saxes, trumpets, trombones, ensemble). You'll also be confronted with a "road map," which includes section repeats, Dal Segnos, and Codas. Bar numbers or letters that act as reference points should also be clearly marked, along with the primary section and ensemble figures.

The problem lies in the fact that arrangers and copyists have different ways of writing a drum part. Unfortunately, one clearly defined system doesn't exist, so it's up to the drummer to determine what the arranger wants and what's most appropriate for the music. With just a basic sketch to go by, you need to depend on your musical instinct and creativity to decide what to play, how to phrase, where to fill, and how to accompany the soloists. **The Big Band Drummer** will help guide you through this formidable task and take some of the mystery out of the procedure as well.

It's About Time

More often than not, the basic rhythmic pattern of an arrangement (jazz, rock, Latin) will be notated in the opening few bars of the drum part. Occasionally a very specific pattern may be notated where it's essential to play the pattern as written. However, most arrangers generally prefer to let you use your imagination and musical creativity in determining what to play, what drums and cymbals to use, and how to best interpret your part.

Some of the ways an arranger may indicate the basic time pattern for a jazz or swing tune are shown below. In each case, example A indicates a four-beat feel, while B requires a two-beat feel. The slash marks in example 5 mean you should ad-lib your own part in accordance with the feel of the arrangement.

Though each of the previous examples could be taken literally, it's doubtful any of them are what the arranger actually wants played. In a typical jazz or swing arrangement, it's almost always safe to assume that the standard jazz time beat with a **triplet feel** is what's required, with either a four feel (A) or a two feel (B).

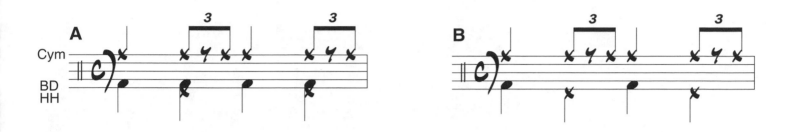

Balance is also extremely important when playing the jazz/swing time pattern. Stronger emphasis should be placed on the ride cymbal and hi-hat, while the bass drum should be **felt** more than heard.

The basic pattern notated on a typical rock or Latin arrangement are also shown below. Once again, most arrangers assume that you will expand on this and ad-lib a part that best complements the music.

In an effort to save time and space, slash marks with a number above them are often used. This simply means to continue the original time pattern—be it jazz, rock, or Latin—for the number of bars indicated.

PLAY 8

Consecutive one-bar repeat signs basically mean the same thing.

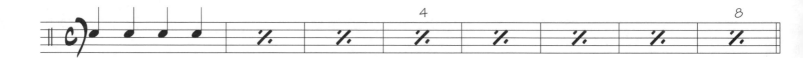

More On Time

Maintaining accurate, solid time is the **first and foremost** responsibility of a big band drummer. Nothing destroys the overall musicality of an arrangement more than a drummer who rushes or drags the tempo.

Big band drummers face an even greater challenge than small-group drummers, due primarily to the larger number of musicians in a big band. In a big band situation, certain entire sections (saxes, trumpets, trombones) may have a tendency to rush or drag the time. Plus, individual players **within** each section may have certain idiosyncrasies when it comes to time. Keeping it all under control when dealing with fourteen to eighteen musicians at the same time can be a formidable task for any drummer.

Improving your time is not the subject of this book, though it's an area all drummers need to address. Two books are highly recommended for a detailed study on the subject: **Time And Drumming** by Lorne Entress, and **The Solid Time Tool Kit** by Ken Myers, both published by Mel Bay Publications.

Phrasing:
The Long and Short of It

Phrasing refers to the components of the drumkit that are used to reinforce and accent the figures in the arrangement. Here's where your musicianship, taste, and listening ability all come into play. Though there are many ways to phrase big band figures, most good players adhere to a few basic principles.

First, big band horn figures are primarily composed of two types of notes: long (sustained) notes, and short (staccato) notes. And though it's been said that long-note phrasing emanates primarily from the sax and trombone sections and short notes from the trumpet section, in actuality, both types of notes can originate from any section of the band at any time. Let's first take a closer look at phrasing long-note figures.

Long-Note Phrasing

Sustained notes are generally best orchestrated on the drumset with the bass drum and crash cymbals. Though the bass drum doesn't fully simulate the full sustain of a long note, it is capable of supplying substantial bottom end and strength to a long-note figure. Many big band drummers use it to reinforce long notes. Cymbals, however, are the primary means of simulating the sustain of a long note.

As a general rule, **quarter notes and notes of longer duration** will require sustained phrasing. Examples A, B, and C below show figures that would require long-note phrasing, indicated by the **dash** above the note. In example D below, notice that **8th notes tied over to longer notes** also require sustained phrasing.

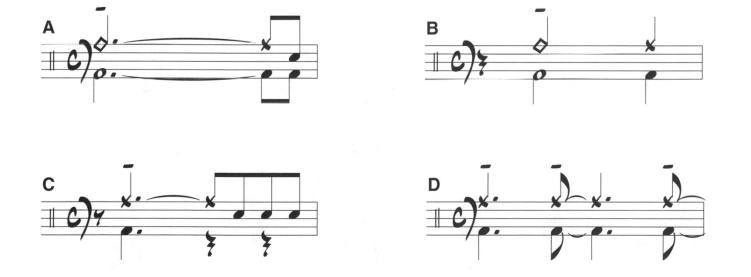

The following page offers an opportunity to practice long-note phrasing. Try using different combinations of cymbals, and practice the examples at different tempos and dynamic levels.

Short-Note Phrasing

Figures that contain **8th notes that stand alone with no notes following, and notes smaller than 8th notes**, are considered short notes.

Many big band players also use the bass drum and cymbals to phrase short notes. However, staccato snare drum accents, rimshots, and fast cymbal crashes are the norm. And though the majority of short-note figures are likely to emanate from the trumpet section, they could originate from any of the band's horn sections. Once again, careful listening is the only way to determine how to most effectively phrase the figures. Here are a few examples of figures best simulated with short-note phrasing, indicated by the **dot** above the note.

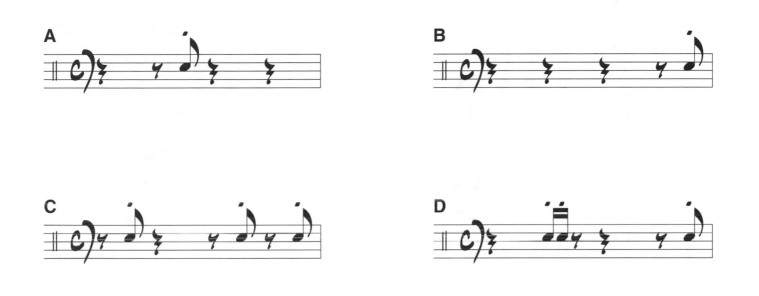

The following examples offer an opportunity to practice short-note phrasing on the drumkit. Here too, try using different combinations of snare drum accents, rimshots, and fast cymbal crashes as you practice these figures.

Note that in the examples that follow, the jazz time pattern is continually played over the figures.

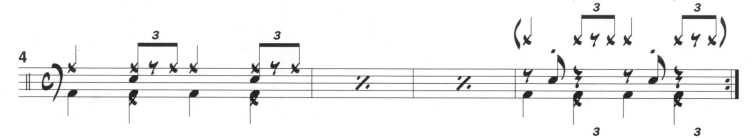

Mixed Long- And Short-Note Phrasing

Quite often, a figure requires a mix of long- and short-note phrasing within the same measure. Section figures (discussed next) often require a combination of long and short phrasing.

In the four examples below, certain notes within the measure require a bit more emphasis (somewhere between a full-on ensemble figure and a more subtle section figure). In these cases, a plus sign (+) will appear above a long note. This means you should lean into the ride cymbal slightly with the shoulder of the stick or lightly strike a crash cymbal to give the note a bit more emphasis and sustain to match the sustain of the long note.

Keep the bass drum going lightly through the figures (more felt than heard) on the 1, 2, 3, and 4 of every measure, with the hi-hat on 2 and 4.

The examples on the following page offer an opportunity to practice mixed long and short note phrasing. Note that leaning into the ride cymbal with the right hand may occasionally alter the ride cymbal pattern slightly. This is perfectly acceptable in big band drumming.

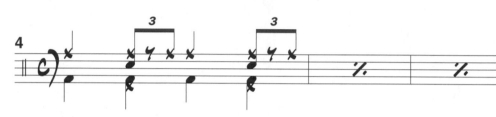

Go Figure:
Understanding Section Figures

Section figures are those rhythmic figures played by only **one**, or possibly two, sections of the band (saxes, trumpets, trombones). Section figures are generally notated *above* the staff with either slash marks (A), repeat signs (B), or a basic time pattern (C) written beneath the figure.

Though section figures usually need to be emphasized with the band, they're usually played in a much more subtle manner than full ensemble figures. Section figures also generally require that you maintain a steady time flow on the ride cymbal and hi-hat, and accent the figures independently of the time pattern so that **the time feel is not interrupted**.

Quite often, cues that indicate what sections of the band (saxes, trumpets, trombones) are playing the figure will be noted on the drum part. These cues can help you determine which components of the drumset you should use to reinforce the figures. For example, trumpet section figures are best accented on snare drum, while the bass drum generally works best for reinforcing sax and trombone section figures.

Note in the three examples below how the trumpet section figures (above the staff) are all played without disturbing the time feel stated on the ride cymbal, bass drum, and hi-hat.

Remember that all 8th-note figures throughout this book are played as jazz 8th notes with a triplet feel.

The following examples demonstrate how the bass drum can reinforce figures played by either the sax or trombone sections, once again, without disturbing the time flow.

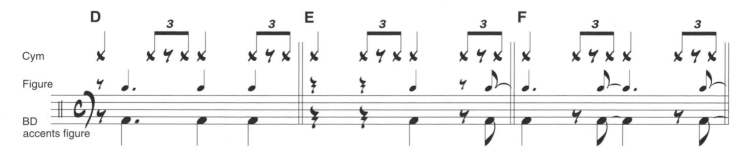

Section Figure Studies

The following pages contain a wide assortment of common section figures usually found in big band arrangements. All of the figures are preceded by three bars of the jazz time beat. Repeat each example numerous times before proceeding to the next, and keep a smooth, steady time flow.

Be sure to practice the examples first using the *snare drum* alone to accent the figures, and then using the **bass drum** alone. Practicing the patterns both ways will help you to become fluent at reinforcing the figures in either manner.

Remember, **the time pattern should not be interrupted** when playing the section figures in the fourth bar. Also, remember to pay careful attention to the phrasing:

* A dash (-) above a note indicates a long, sustained phrasing.
* A dot (.) above a note indicates short, staccato phrasing.
* A plus sign (+) above any *long note* means you should lean into the ride cymbal slightly with the shoulder of the stick, or lightly strike a crash cymbal, to give the note a bit more emphasis and sustain. In some cases, this may affect the jazz cymbal pattern, altering it from:

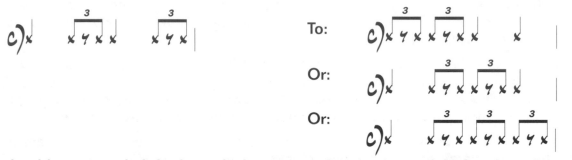

The bass drum should continue lightly through the section figures (more felt than heard) on the 1, 2, 3, and 4 of every measure, with the hi-hat on 2 and 4.

Finally, since there are different ways of notating same-sounding figures, some of the examples may sound similar to others, but be notated differently. It's important to be familiar with the various ways in which the same rhythmic pattern may appear on your part.

Go Figure **29**

Understanding Ensemble Figures

Ensemble figures are rhythmic figures played by the *entire* band. Ensemble figures are generally notated directly on the staff to distinguish them from section figures, though inconsistencies among arrangers and copyists may occur. Careful listening is essential.

Ensemble figures usually need to be emphasized *strongly*, and can be orchestrated around the kit in various ways. Here are four examples of possible orchestrations. **A)** Snare drum alone. **B)** Snare drum and bass drum. **C)** Snare drum, bass drum, and cymbals. **D)** A combination of the above.

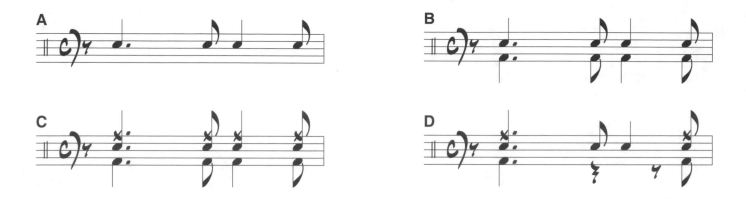

Unlike section figures, the time pattern generally *will be interrupted* during ensemble figures so that the figures can be accented using the major components of the kit. Exceptions to this are figures containing half notes and dotted half notes, or when an ensemble figure is made up of only short 8th notes. In these cases, dropping the time pattern out completely would result in a very awkward disruption of the time flow. Here are a few examples of where you would *not* want to stop the time pattern through the figure.

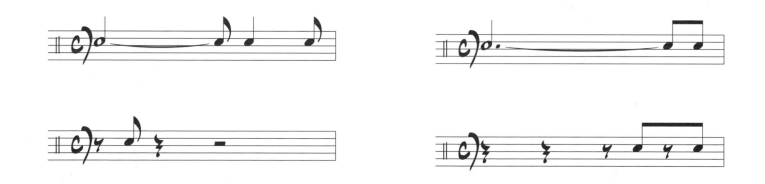

For practice purposes, all of the ensemble figures on the following pages have been orchestrated using example C above (snare drum, bass drum, and cymbal in unison).

Bear in mind that in an actual performance situation, you wouldn't necessarily orchestrate every ensemble figure with all three components of the kit. Careful listening to the ensemble is critical, since many factors come into play in determining what orchestration of an ensemble figure best fits the music. Those factors include tempo, volume, the manner in which the horns phrase the figure (long and short notes), how much emphasis of the figure is required, and what orchestration works best *musically*.

After working through the pages that follow as written, try experimenting with different orchestrations of the same figure, using the examples above as a guide.

Ensemble Figure Studies

The following pages contain the same figures used in our study of section figures. Once again, all of the figures are preceded by three bars of the jazz time beat. Repeat each line numerous times before proceeding to the next, and be conscious of keeping a smooth, steady time flow. It's also a good idea to practice all of the examples at slow, medium, and fast tempos.

Though all of the figures have been orchestrated using snare drum, bass drum, and cymbal, feel free to experiment with optional orchestrations of the figures as you work your way through the material.

As with the section figures that preceded this material, there are various ways of notating same-sounding figures. Therefore, some of the examples will sound similar to others, but will be notated differently. It's essential to be aware of the various ways in which the same figure could appear on the drum part.

Finally, remember that all of the figures on the following pages are to be played with a jazz-triplet feel.

Two-Bar Figures

More often than not, section and ensemble figures do not appear in simple one-bar groupings on a big band drum part. It's quite common for a series of figures to extend over two, four, or even eight bars. The following examples are designed to help you develop a feel for two-bar section and ensemble figures.

Two-Bar Section Figures

Two-Bar Ensemble Figures

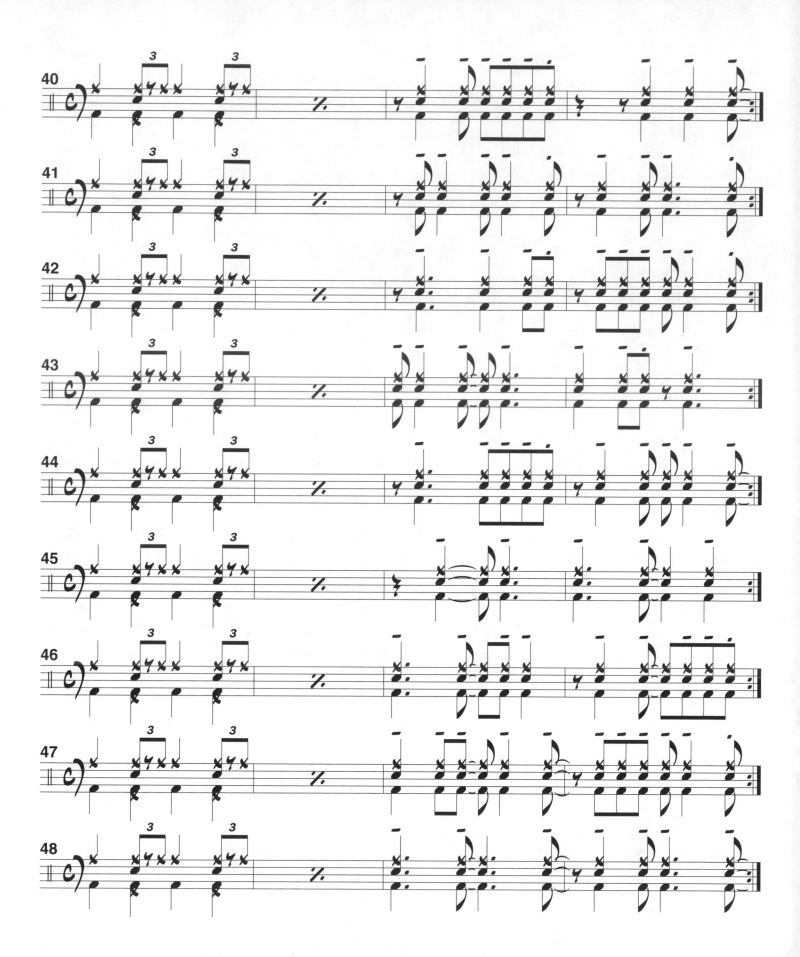

Four-Bar Section Figures

Four bars of time, followed by a four-bar section figure phrase.

Four-Bar Ensemble Figures

Four bars of time, followed by a four-bar ensemble figure phrase.

6

7

8

9

10

Fillin' In The Gaps:
Understanding Fills

A fill is a rhythmic pattern of indeterminate length, played just prior to a horn section or ensemble figure. The purpose of a fill is twofold: 1) to set the band up for the figure and lead them into it, and 2) to add color, intensity, and rhythmic interest to the arrangement.

Fills can range from a simple, strategically placed four-stroke ruff to one that is a full bar in length. However, taste and musical sensitivity are essential. Overplaying fills can be pretty ineffective, and those that come off as mini drum solos are rarely musical and often out of place.

Listen to some of the great big band drummers to get an idea of how fills are used to add color and interest to the music.

Upbeat Fills

One of the most common places to play a fill is just before an upbeat figure (figures that occur on the "&" of 1, 2, 3, and 4).

We'll begin our study by first playing fills before dotted quarter notes on the "&" of 1. This will be followed by fills before the "&" of 2, the "&" of 3, and the "&" of 4. Each exercise is preceded by three bars of the jazz time beat.

The first fill is a four-stroke ruff, followed by a two-8th-note fill, a triplet fill, and a 16th-note fill. Note how as the duration of the fill increases, it's moved further back into the preceding bar of time. *Anticipation* is the key word when playing fills that lead into figures.

The following fills have been written for snare drum only. However, feel free to experiment by moving the lengthier fills between different drums and cymbals, and creating your own combinations and patterns. Also be sure to practice these exercises at various tempos.

Upbeat Of One

8th-Note Fill

Two-8th-Note Fill

Triplet Fill

Four-16th-Note Fill

Upbeat Of Two

8th-Note Fill

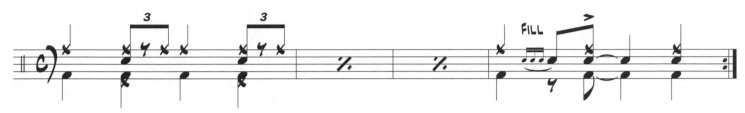

Two-8th-Note Fill

Triplet Fill

Four-16th-Note Fill

Upbeat Of Three

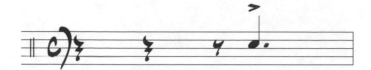

8th-Note Fill

Two-8th-Note Fill

Triplet Fill

Four-16th-Note Fill

Upbeat Of Four

8th-Note Fill

Two-8th-Note Fill

Triplet Fill

Four-16th-Note Fill

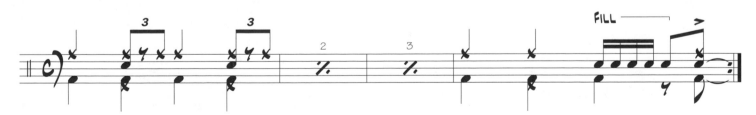

More Fills

The following fills demonstrate the use of more complex rhythms.

Upbeat Of One

Upbeat Of Two

Upbeat Of Three

Upbeat Of Four

Fills Within The Figure

A common technique used by most big band drummers is to play fills "between" the notes of a figure. Here are a few examples.

Figure:

1
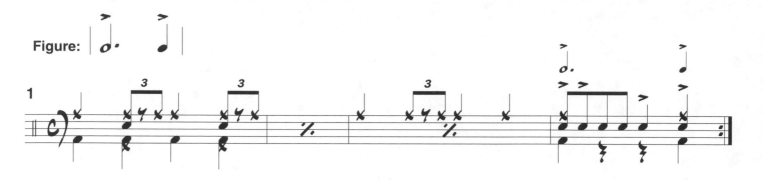

Figure:

2
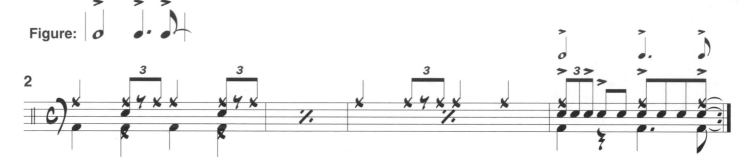

Figure:

3
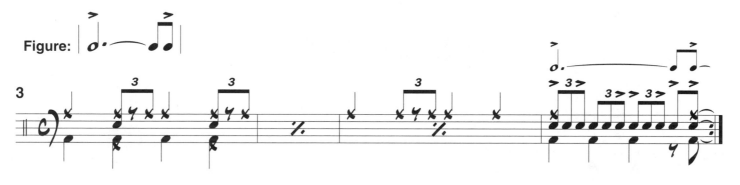

Figure:

4
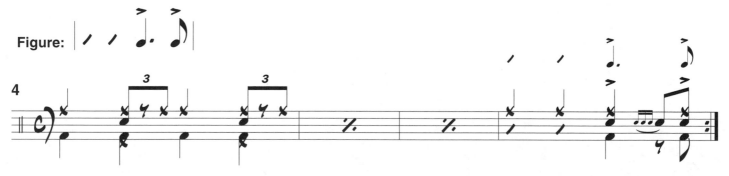

Figure:

5
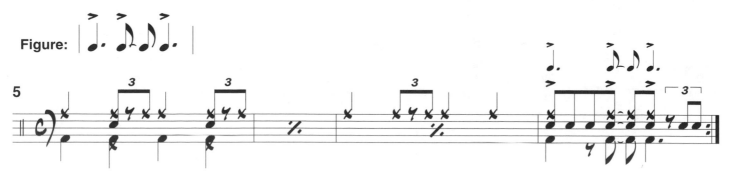

Adding Fills

The following two pages are good practice for working fills in among *one-bar* ensemble figures. Use your imagination and create rhythmic fills that utilize various components of the kit.

The next twenty examples will help you develop a feel for working fills in among *two-bar* ensemble figures. Avoid overplaying, maintain good taste, and keep solid time.

The Road Map: What It All Means

The signs and symbols arrangers and copyists use in an average big band arrangement comprise a language all its own. Before you can safely approach a typical big band drum part, it's essential to be *totally* familiar with the language.

The following pages demonstrate the most common signs and symbols you're likely to run up against on a big band drum part. It's important to learn them all.

Tempo & Pulse

Tempo Markings: ♩ = 120

The number 120 means that the arrangement will be played at 120 beats per minute.

Slash Marks:

Slash marks are a shorthand means to indicate playing time in the musical style of the arrangement.

Pulsation:

"4 FEEL"

"4 Feel" means to play the section with a feel of four beats to every bar.

"2 FEEL"

"2 Feel" means to play the section with a feel of two beats to every bar.

Repeat Signs

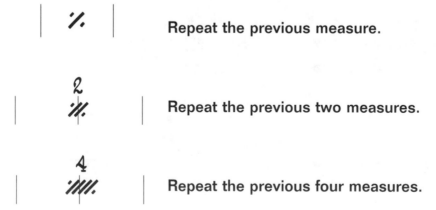

Repeat the previous measure.

Repeat the previous two measures.

Repeat the previous four measures.

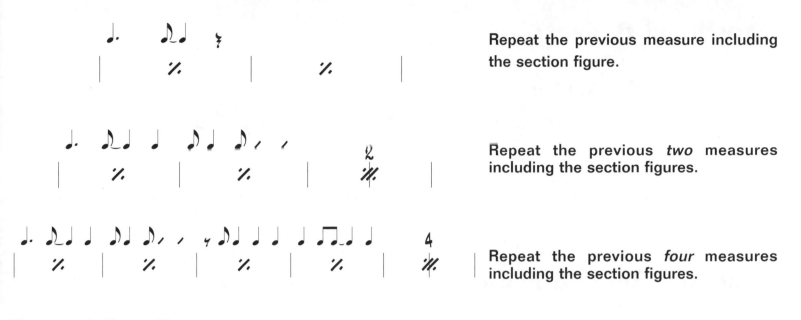

Repeat the previous measure including the section figure.

Repeat the previous *two* measures including the section figures.

Repeat the previous *four* measures including the section figures.

Dotted Bar Repeats

Repeat all of the measures between the dotted bar lines.

Extended One-Bar Repeats

Repeat the figure in the first measure for the number of times indicated (eight repeats).

Extended Section Repeats

PLAY 3X's

"Play 3X's" means to repeat the eight-bar section between the dotted-bar repeats a total of three times.

Shorthand Repeat

"Play 8" in both of the examples above is an abbreviated means of indicating eight bars of time in the style of the arrangement.

First And Second Endings

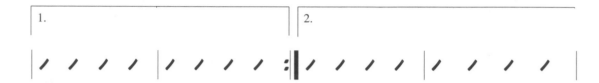

The first time through, play the first ending and repeat. The second time through, skip the first ending and play the second ending.

Da Capo

Go back to the beginning of the arrangement.

D.S. al Coda

Dal Segno

Coda ⊕

Play through the arrangement until you reach the *D.S. al Coda*. Return to the *Dal Segno* sign. Play through again until you reach the *Coda* sign. Then go directly to the ending *Coda* section.

Solos, Fills, And Rests

Solo

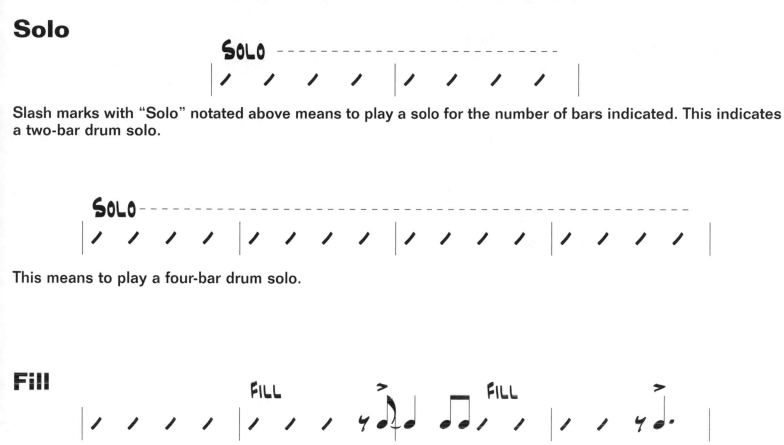

Slash marks with "Solo" notated above means to play a solo for the number of bars indicated. This indicates a two-bar drum solo.

This means to play a four-bar drum solo.

Fill

"Fill" notated above the staff means the arranger wants you to lead the band into the figures that follow, and fill-in the spaces between the figures.

Tacet

"Tacet" means *do not* play a section of the arrangement for the number of measures indicated.

Rest Bars

This means *do not* play for the number of bars indicated above the sign

Dynamics And Tempo Signs

pp = very soft
p = soft
mp = moderately soft
mf = moderately loud
f = loud
ff = very loud

Crescendo

Gradually increase the volume through the number of bars indicated.

Decrescendo

Gradually decrease the volume through the number of bars indicated.

Ritard

RIT. -

Gradually get slower through the number of bars indicated.

Accelerando

ACCEL. -

Gradually get faster through the number of bars indicated.

Fermata

The fermata sign means to sustain the note until the leader cuts the note off with a hand signal.

Applying It All

The final pages of this book contain six sample drum charts that utilize most of the material previously studied. Each chart is preceded by a brief analysis that highlights key points. After you've mastered the individual elements, try playing through the chart from beginning to end without stopping. Hopefully you've absorbed all of the techniques that make for good big band drumming by this point and are ready to *apply* it all in this final section of the book. If you're unsure about anything in the sample charts that follow, go back and review previous chapters.

Chart #1

The first thing to take notice of on this chart is the arranger's indication that this is a bright swing tune played at 160 beats per minute. Next, take a good look at the road map, which is a little more involved here. Along with the three eight-bar section repeats at the intro, letter C, and letter F, pay special attention to the D.S. and Coda signs. The D.S. al Coda appears at the end of letter H, taking you back to the sign at letter A. From there, play through until you reach the Coda sign at letter B, and then go directly to the Coda at the bottom of the page. It's always essential to be familiar with the road map ahead of time to avoid surprises. There's nothing more embarrassing than finding yourself in one place on your part while the rest of the band is at another.

Note that this arrangement begins with an eight-bar piano solo that repeats. Though straight quarter notes are written for the time pattern, it's safe to assume that the jazz time beat with a "four" feel (indicated by the bass drum part) is what the arranger actually wants played.

Be aware of the section figures at letter A, followed by the sixteen-bar trumpet solo at B and the eight-bar sax solo at letter C that repeats. At letter D we find some basic trombone section figures that the arranger wants you to be aware of. After the two-bar rest at letter E, note the instructions to play fills between the ensemble figures. Also note the two-bar drum solo at the very end of letter E.

After the repeat of letter F, be especially aware of the mix of ensemble *and* section figures that run through letter G. An eight-bar bass solo at letter H leads directly to the D.S. al Coda previously discussed.

The Coda has some strong ensemble figures, with several drum solos interspersed. The final drum solo leads to the fermata on the fourth beat. That note is sustained until a hand signal from the leader cuts the band off.

Chart #1

Chart #2

In this chart the arranger is being a bit more specific about what he wants played. A straight-8th rock feel is clearly notated at the top of the chart, complete with afterbeats on 2 and 4.

More importantly, notice that the bass drum line is written out. This indicates that something is happening musically in the arrangement that requires reinforcement of that rhythm. Careful listening to the band will help you determine just how much emphasis is required.

The same pattern continues at letter A, along with a 16th-note section figure that's repeated once. At letter C we find a three-bar ensemble figure that obviously needs to be played note for note, but without losing the overall rock feel of the tune.

An eight-bar trumpet solo follows at letter D, but be aware that letter D is actually played three times (3X's). Also, note the two section figures after letter E, both of which are repeated.

At letter F the arrangement changes to a "samba feel." The bass drum notation offers a sample of what the arranger is looking for.

There's no indication regarding what to play on the rest of the kit at this point, so you can pretty much ad-lib what you feel is appropriate for the music. Just remember to catch the ensemble figure one bar before letter G.

At letter G, we find a four-bar run of section figures. Though it can be somewhat difficult to tell what section or sections of the band are playing these figures, close listening will help you determine how strong these figures need to be. Also, note the first- and second-ending repeats of letter G, as well as the one-bar solo at the first ending.

The final four bars of this arrangement are written as strong ensemble figures with fills interspersed. It's probably best to keep the fills as simple as possible, keeping your primary focus on accurately executing the important closing figures with the band.

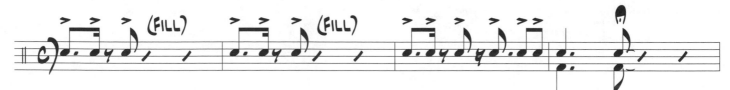

Chart #2

Chart #3

The first thing to be aware of here is that the arrangement kicks right off with a six-bar intro that includes some strong ensemble figures. The time pattern—beginning two bars before letter A—is notated more accurately than normal, and is often written in this manner. The correct interpretation, however, is a triplet time feel.

At letter A we find some basic section figures with "fill" written in at several points. Note the two double-bar repeats at letter B, along with the Dal Segno sign, which you'll return to later in the chart.

Letter C contains more fills dropped in between section figures, along with a "1st X only" indication at the double-bar repeat. This tells you that during the second playing of this section, following the D.S. repeat, letter C is *not* played a second time.

After a one-bar drum solo at the end of letter D, a very important twelve-bar ensemble section appears at letter E. The arranger has even written a bass drum line to match the figures. Many arrangers and copyists notate ensemble figures in this manner. And though most big band drummers would not take the bass drum part literally, they *would* take it to mean that this ensemble section requires heavy emphasis. Be aware that the first four bars of letter E repeat, while the D.S. al Coda at the twelfth bar takes you quickly back to letter B.

The Coda sign at the end of letter C brings you to the Coda section at the bottom of the page. Several bars of section and ensemble figures lead up to a one-bar solo just before the final measure.

Chart #3

Chart #4

This arrangement is in 3/4, but played in "one" for more of a bright, jazz-waltz feel.

After an eight-bar introduction, the full ensemble kicks in at letter A. These figures need to be played as written, but without losing the jazz-waltz pulsation. The bass drum notated on the first beat of every measure is an indication that the "one" feel needs to be maintained throughout this section.

Following the second playing of letter A, there's a thirty-two-bar trumpet solo immediately followed by an alto sax solo at letter C, with section figures above the solo. The double-bar repeat tells us that letter C is also played twice.

The four-bar rest at letter D leads into a sixteen-bar tenor sax solo, which repeats (Play 2X's), followed by a sixteen-bar trombone solo that's played three times (Play 3X's). Would it have been more logical to indicate the tenor solo at thirty-two bars and the trombone solo at fourty-eight? It certainly would have. But arrangers and copyists don't always think in logical terms when notating drum parts, so it's important to be prepared for anything.

Letter E is the last critical point in the arrangement requiring accurate interpretation. The quarter rests in the first four bars tell us that the entire band cuts out at these points, so the fills stand alone and are almost mini solos. Accurate counting is absolutely essential here. Also note that the first ending contains a longer, eight-bar solo.

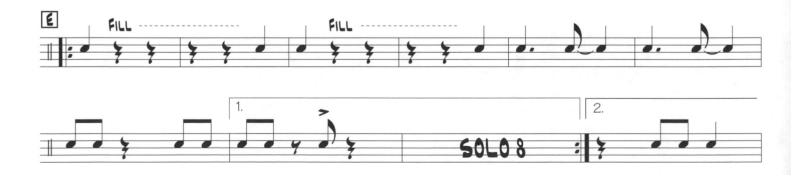

Practice this chart a bit slower at first, and gradually work it up to the recommended tempo.

Chart #4

Chart #5

Chart #5 is a Latin American arrangement with a mambo feel. A basic mambo cowbell rhythm is shown at letter A, though the bell of a cymbal would be an appropriate substitute. The bass drum part is written in "two," and the tempo marking tells us that the tune moves along at a relatively brisk pace.

The written mambo pattern is very basic (ex. A), so you'd most likely be expected to expand upon it. Example B below shows one possibility, using rimclicks, tom-toms, and a slightly altered bass drum part.

Bear in mind that since this arrangement is in the Latin vein, all of the 8th-note figures are interpreted as *straight 8th notes* and are played exactly as written. The first figure appears at the end of letter A.

The basic mambo pattern continues behind the trombone solo at letter B. The ensemble figures that follow need to be played strongly, while maintaining the Latin feel. The thirty-two-bar trumpet solo at letter C is followed by more section figures at letter D. Still more section figures follow the piano solo at letter E, which leads us to letter F. Be aware of the solos and fills that fall between the ensemble figures in this section, along with the D.S. al Coda sign that takes us back to letter B.

The Coda begins with a run of section figures that leads into a four-bar ensemble figure that needs to be executed with the band as written. The unison bass drum part simply tells us that heavy emphasis of these figures is required.

Chart #5

Chart #6

This last chart is an uptempo swing arrangement that's an exercise in moving back and forth between "two" and "four" feels. The tune starts out in two, and though the time pattern is notated with straight 8ths, it should be played with a triplet feel.

The arrangement changes to a four feel at letter A, followed by eight bars of section figures and a one-bar solo. A sixteen-bar sax solo runs through letter B, while C is actually a thirty-two-bar trumpet solo, with the last two bars being ensemble figures that lead out of the solo.

At letter D, we find some ensemble figures that call for fills and others that do not. Note the difference in notation between the first two bars of letter D and later bars where "fill" is suggested. Letter D repeats via first and second endings, both of which consist of two-bar drum solos.

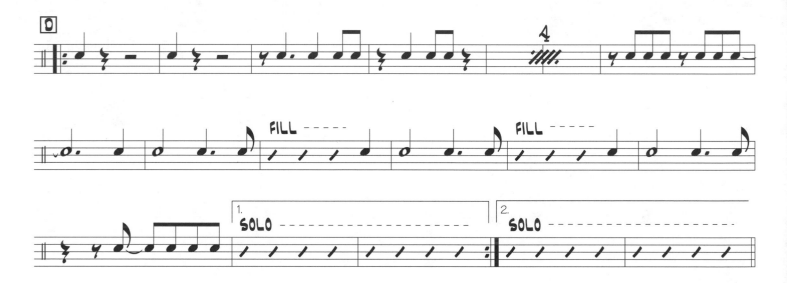

The arrangement returns to a two feel at letter E, followed by four bars of solo. At letter F the tune once again resorts to a four feel, and ends with more ensemble figures and one last solo bar just before the final measure.

Chart #6

Big Band Drummer's Listening Guide

Anything By	As Performed With
Chick Webb	The Chick Webb Band
Papa Jo Jones	Count Basie
Sonny Greer	Duke Ellington
Jimmy Crawford	Jimmy Lunceford
Ray McKinley	Glenn Miller
Cliff Leeman	Artie Shaw, Tommy Dorsey, Charlie Barnet
Gene Krupa	Benny Goodman, Gene Krupa Band
Dave Tough	Tommy Dorsey, Woody Herman
Buddy Rich	Artie Shaw, Tommy Dorsey, Buddy Rich Band
Tiny Kahn	Chubby Jackson Band
Shadow Wilson	Count Basie
Stan Levey	Stan Kenton, Woody Herman
Don Lamond	Woody Herman
Sonny Igoe	Woody Herman
Shelly Manne	Stan Kenton
Louie Bellson	Duke Ellington, Tommy Dorsey, Harry James, Louie Bellson Band
Sonny Payne	Count Basie
Jake Hanna	Woody Herman
Sam Woodyard	Duke Ellington
Harold Jones	Count Basie
Stu Martin	Maynard Ferguson
Ed Shaughnessy	Doc Severinsen
Frankie Dunlop	Maynard Ferguson
Rufus Jones	Duke Ellington
Mel Lewis	Gerry Mulligan, Mel Lewis/Thad Jones Band
Butch Miles	Count Basie
Peter Erskine	Stan Kenton, Maynard Ferguson
John Riley	Vanguard Jazz Orchestra
Dave Weckl	GRP Big Band